Decorate your star so that it will show on stage. Glittery things that catch the light are good.

2 Low-flying star

The star that led the wise men to Bethlehem hung low over one little house. Inside they found Jesus and his mother Mary.
   Make a beautiful star to hang in your house for Christmas.

1 Copy the six-pointed star onto card and cut it out. Use this shape to draw three stars on card and cut them out.

2 Fold each in half from top point to bottom point. Unfold and paint. Leave to dry.

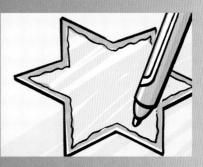

3 Outline the edges of all three stars on both sides, using a thick felt-tip pen.

4 Lay out your beads to make a sparkly hanging. Thread from the top bead down to the bottom bead (or bell) then thread back up to the top knot.

5 Tape the thread to the bottom point of one star. Make a thread loop for the top, to hang the star.

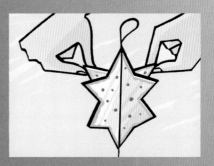

6 Spread glue over the back of each star, fit together and spread the points prettily.

Be very careful to cut all your stars exactly like this, so they glue together neatly.

For easy
threading,
dip one end
of your bead
thread in
glue and
leave to go
dry and stiff
like a
needle.

3 Starry angels

The Christmas story tells of angels. They sang in the night sky above Bethlehem on the night Jesus was born.

Make a starry angel halo to wear.

1 Cut a strip of card long enough to fit round your head with an overlap. Then cut lots of star shapes and glue them on.

2 Bend the band into a circle that fits on your head without slipping. Tape or staple to fix.

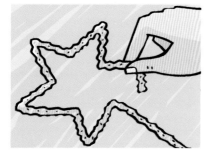

3 Zig-zag fold a glittery pipe cleaner so you have ten bends in all. Twist the ends together and arrange the bends into a star shape.

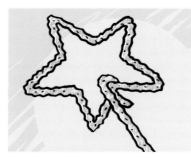

4 Bend another pipe cleaner to clasp the bottom of the star. Then tape the other end to the halo band. Make as many stick-up stars as you like!

4 Heaven to earth

Christmas is about all the blessings of heaven coming to earth. Let this shooting star be a reminder of Christmas blessings.

1 Copy the star shape and the tail shape onto plain card. Cut them out so you can draw round them on coloured card.

2 For each shooting star, draw two star shapes and three tail shapes. Trim one of your stars so it is a tiny bit smaller than the other.

3 Arrange the tail shapes so they overlap. Glue them together then decorate them with pens and stick on stars.

4. Glue the smaller star on top of the other star. Glue it onto the tail.

5 The legend of the Christmas tree

There are many Christmas tree legends. One links to the Bible story about King Herod's soldiers coming to kill Jesus.

Mary and Joseph fled with their baby boy. When night came, they sheltered under a fir tree. A white frost covered the tree with icicles. The soldiers passed by but did not see the little family hidden behind the sparkling ice.

Make this icicle star for the top of your tree.

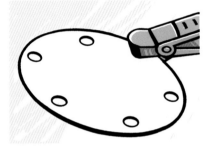

1 Cut a circle of card. Mark six evenly spaced points around the edge and punch holes.

2 Decorate the card with pens, stick-on jewels and glitter glue.

3 Push a pipe cleaner in through one hole and out through the opposite hole. Make sure the ends stick out the same length. Do the same with the other pairs of holes.

4 Trim the ends of the pipe cleaners, except for one which you leave long to tie to the tree.

5 Thread beads onto the sparkly ends, or glue on snowballs or cut-out card shapes.

6 More icicle stars

These star decorations are so quick to make you could cover your tree in them!

1 Make a circle shape, about 3cm across. Punch five equally spaced holes around the edge.

2 Use this shape to draw as many more circles as you like, and to mark where the holes go. Cut out the circles and punch the holes.

3 Cut pipe cleaners into 6cm lengths. Thread them through a pair of holes like this to make a star pattern.

4 Trim the ends of your pipe cleaners so they match. Add a hanging loop of thread through one hole. Do steps 3 and 4 with all your circles.

You can make icicle stars with five points or six points.

7 Starry cards

Send Christmas greetings to those you love with these starry cards.

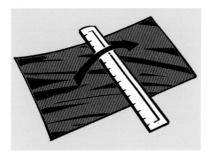

1 Cut a rectangle of card 20cm x 10cm. Mark the middle point in each of the long sides. Lay a ruler from mark to mark and fold the card in half along its edge.

2 Tear contrasting paper into ragged squares about 9cm x 9cm. Glue on the front of the card.

3 Ask a grown-up to help you prepare a potato printer: cut a potato in half and press a star cookie cutter into one flat surface. Cut away the edges of the potato up to the cutter. Then remove the cutter.

4 Spread a thin layer of paint on a flat plate. Dip your printer in the paint, blot it on a scrap of paper, then print it on your card.

Use different sorts of paper and different arrangements of stars to make all your cards a little bit different – and very special.

8 Starry gift wrap

Make lots of special paper to wrap the special gifts you are going to give.

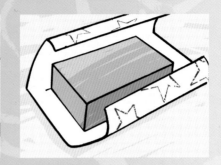

1 Paint sheets of plain white paper. Using a sponge to apply the paint is quick and looks stylish. Leave to dry.

2 Spread a thin layer of paint on a flat plate. Dip a star-shaped cookie cutter in the paint, blot it on a scrap of paper, then print on your card.

3 Wrap a box: measure the right width as the height of the box and the width of the box and about 1cm more. Cut your paper this size.

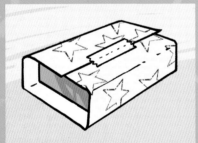

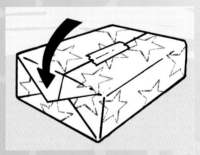

4 Measure the right length as wrapping round the box with an overlap. Now centre the box on the paper and wrap. Tape in place.

5 Check the box is centred as you squash the short sides in. Crease.

6 Fold the bottom flap up and the top flap over it. Tape.

Mix a little white (PVA) glue with water-based paints for this project. The glue will stop the paint flaking and cracking at the edges of your parcels.

There are ideas
for gift labels on
the next page!

9 Gift tags

Add a starry gift tag to say who the gift is for. Let them know you think they're a star!

1 Copy the shape on the back of the book shown here onto card and cut it out. Mark the edge that goes along the fold.

2 Cut a rectangle of card about 20cm x 10cm and fold it in half. Lay the shape on it, matching the correct edge to the fold.

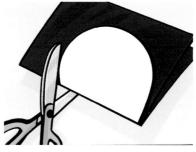

3 Draw round the shape and cut out the tag. Then punch a hole in the corner by the fold.

4 On tissue paper, draw round a tumbler to mark circles about 9cm across. Cut them out.

5 Fold each circle in half and then in half again. Snip the folded edges as shown to make starry lace.

6 Unfold. Glue the starry lace onto the tag, Then add a ribbon or string to attach to the parcel ribbon.

You can have lots of fun finding different ways to fold and snip to make all kinds of starry lace.

10 Star cookies

Star food, star taste – and great for sharing and for giving as a gift.
Ask a grown-up before you begin any cooking. Let them deal with the actual baking, and ask them to turn the oven to 180°C/gas mark 4.

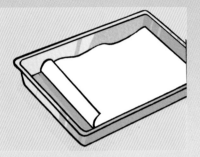

1 Wash your hands. Line a baking tray with parchment.

2 Put one egg white in a bowl and whisk until it is stiff. Add 100g caster sugar and whisk for about 3 minutes. Put about a quarter of the mix aside in a small bowl.

3 Then add 100g ground almonds and 1 teaspoon of cinnamon to the main mix. Add more ground almonds till you have a stiff ball of mix.

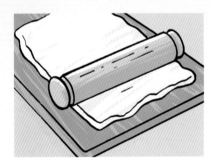

4 Lay baking parchment on a clean work surface. Sprinkle with cornflour. Put the almond mixture ball on top and sprinkle with more cornflour. Roll out to 5mm thick.

5 Use a star cutter to cut out stars. Lift the shapes onto the tray. Gather any scraps of mix and reroll to make more stars.

6 Spoon a tiny blob of the egg white mix which was put aside earlier into the centre of each biscuit.

7 Bake the biscuits for 8–10 minutes, or until they just turn brown. Let the stars cool for a few minutes on the tray, then lift them onto a wire rack to cool completely.

11 Star cookie box

This clever package is perfect for keeping your star cookies unsquashed – and makes a very glamorous gift.

1 Take a paper bowl and mark the place for six evenly spaced holes around the rim. Punch holes through.

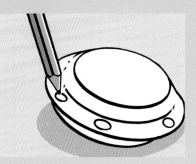

2 Lay the bowl on another and mark the place for six matching holes. Punch through.

3 Now paint the outside of each of the bowls and leave to dry. Then decorate with glitter glue and glitz – especially the lid bowl.

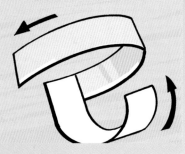

4 Cut two strips of paper about 2cm x 17cm and glue at right angles to each other. Fold the right hand strip to the left, and downward strip up.

5 Now fold the left strip to the right, and the upward strip down. Keep folding till the strip is used up. Glue the ends of your paper spring.

6 Cut two matching stars, using shapes from the back of this book. Trim one to be slightly smaller than the other and glue it on top.

7 Glue the double star onto one end of the paper spring and glue the spring to the lid bowl.

8 Put your gift inside one bowl and the lid bowl on top. Match up the holes and thread with ribbon.

Twists of pipe cleaner could be used instead of ribbon to hold the two halves of this package together.

If you are putting cookies in the package, first wrap them in cling film or greaseproof paper.

12 Star sweetie box

Clever paper folding – called origami in Japanese – makes a box with starry points. Fill it with sweets for the Christmas table.

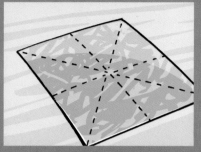

1 Cut a perfect square of about 25cm x 25cm. Fold diagonally corner to corner and crease, then unfold and repeat with the other corners. Then fold in half and unfold. Then fold in half the other way.

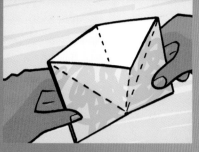

2 Hold the lower corners as shown and squeeze into the shape as shown.

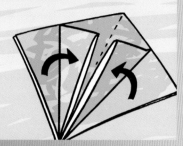

3 Place the paper with the open ends towards you. Fold the left and right corners of the top layer into a kite shape. Turn the paper over and do the same again.

4 Open out the flap and squash flat. Do this to all four flaps.

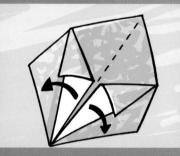

5 Fold the flaps in like this on one side. Turn the paper over and do the same on the other side.

6 You have a shape like this. Fold the corners back as shown. Turn the paper over and repeat on the other side.

7 Fold the base down. Crease towards you and away from you.

8 Fold the flaps open.

This paper was brushed with gold on one side. The other was finger painted in swirls of green and blue.

Stick on
jewels and
add sparkle.

13 All-join-in star

This star has 12 spikes. Everyone can learn to make a spike – or two or three or more! – and then put them together.

1 Cut 12 squares of coloured paper, each 14cm x 14cm. Fold and unfold like this. Then fold the corners to the centre.

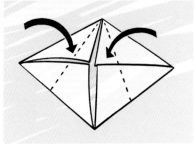

2 Now fold the sides in to make a kite shape.

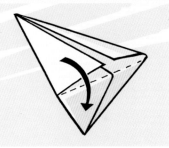

3 Fold the lower part under as shown.

4 Fold right to left as shown.

5 Tuck the spikes together.

14 Star toy

Use lots of glitz to make this star really sparkle as it spins.
Let everyone have a turn at your Christmas party – or help them
make their own toy to take away.

1 Cut a circle about
12cm across in thick
card. Paint both sides
and leave to dry.

2 Draw a big six-pointed
star in the centre on one
side. Press a pin through
each point then draw a
star exactly the same on
the other side with the
points at the pin marks.

3 Brush glue inside the
star outline and fill with
glitter. Add glitz around
the edge for even more
sparkle! Allow to dry.
Turn over and decorate
the other star in a plain
colour.

4 Mark two places
exactly opposite each
other as shown and
punch a hole in each.

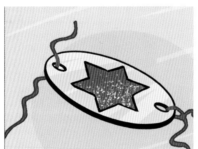

5 Thread wool as shown
and knot close to the
edge of the card.

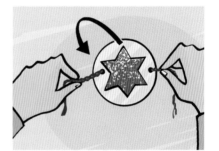

6 Hold the disc by the
wool 'ends' and flip it
many times to twist the
wool. Then pull on each
side to untwist it – and
watch the disc spin and
glitter.

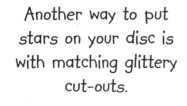

Another way to put
stars on your disc is
with matching glittery
cut-outs.

I5 Window star

Stained glass windows in churches are lit by sunlight and moonlight. Create the same effect in your window on Christmas night – and through all the Christmas season.

1 Cut six narrow strips of black card, all the same length.

2 Take three and arrange into a perfect triangle. Trim the ends to a point. Glue in place.

3 Draw around the triangle on coloured tissue paper and cut a paper triangle. Trim it to be a little smaller all round, and glue it in your card triangle.

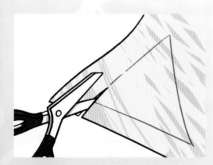

4 Do the same with the other three strips and another colour of tissue paper.

5 Overlap the triangles to make a six-pointed star and glue together.

Use sticky putty to fix your star to a window.

16 Star light, star bright

*My candle burns; its tiny light
shines to make this
dark place bright.
My candle burns,
a flame of love,
shining up to heaven above.*

1 Take a plain flowerpot
and matching saucer.
Brush all over with gesso
or white acrylic paint.
Leave to dry.

2 Paint the pots in bright
colours. Leave to dry.

3 If you wish, cut a
star-shaped hole in a
piece of strong paper.
Press it against the side
of the pot and use as a
stencil.

4 Brush white glue
thickly on the edge of
the pot and the saucer.
Dip the gluey edges into
a saucerful of glitter.

Block the hole in the pot
with a piece of card and fill
with sand before pushing
a candle in firmly. Ask a
grown-up to take charge of
lighting the candle and
putting it out safely.